writers
and their times

John Steinbeck
and the Great Depression

Alison Morretta

Cavendish Square

New York

For Richie and Ro-Ro

Published in 2015 by Cavendish Square Publishing, LLC
243 5th Avenue, Suite 136, New York, NY 10016

Copyright © 2015 by Cavendish Square Publishing, LLC

First Edition

Library of Congress Cataloging-in-Publication Data

Morretta, Alison.
John Steinbeck and the Great Depression / Alison Morretta.
pages cm. — (Writers and their times)
Includes bibliographical references and index.
ISBN 978-1-62712-812-4 (hardcover) ISBN 978-1-62712-814-8 (ebook)
1. Steinbeck, John, 1902-1968—Criticism and interpretation. 2. Depressions—1929—United States. I. Title.

PS3537.T3234Z76 2015
813'.52—dc23

2014003269

Editorial Director: Dean Miller
Editor: Kristen Susienka
Senior Copy Editor: Wendy A. Reynolds
Art Director: Jeffrey Talbot
Designer: Amy Greenan
Production Manager: Jennifer Ryder-Talbot
Production Editor: David McNamara
Photo Research: J8 Media

writers
and their times

Contents

Introduction

The "I" and the "We"

ohn Steinbeck lived and wrote during many periods of
great change in America. During his lifetime, Steinbeck
saw World War I, the boom times of the 1920s, the hard
times of the Great Depression, World War II, the Cold War,
and the Vietnam War. While he is best known for his
Depression-era novels, he was also a social historian of many
of the other events that shaped American history during the
early and mid-twentieth century. Steinbeck was interested in
the struggles of the common man and the relationship of the
individual to the group. He also never lost his passion for the
land of his birth, California, and the natural landscape of his
home state is as much a character in many of his novels as the
individuals who inhabit them.

Steinbeck's interests were varied and he had an insatiable
curiosity for knowledge that kept him a lifelong student of the
world. He was a student of science, specifically **ecology** and the
way organisms were inextricably linked with their environment.
He grew increasingly involved in politics in his later years and

A family of Dust Bowl migrants from Oklahoma work in the pea fields near Nipomo, California, in the 1930s.

was something of a philosopher as well. Steinbeck's **phalanx theory** is integral to many of his works, especially his late-1930s Depression novels. Steinbeck believed that a group made up of individual units takes on the characteristics of an individual and is stronger than the sum of its parts. To understand this theory is to understand the way the writer viewed and interpreted the world around him. In a letter to a friend, when he was first formulating the idea, he wrote:

> [T]he group is an individual as boundaried, as diagnosable, as dependent on its units and as independent of its units' individual natures, as the human unit, or man, is dependent on his cells and yet is independent of them … The greatest group unit, that is the whole race, has qualities which the individual lacks entirely.

Steinbeck did not see the world in terms of good and evil. He believed that people, like other creatures in the natural world, acted as they were meant to act given their environment. He distinguished between the "I" and the "we"—the individual men and women that made up a group, and the group itself.

It is not surprising, given Steinbeck's time and place, that he would become a keen observer of the individual versus the group mentality. The wars he lived through bred armies made up of soldiers; the boom and bust leading to the Depression defined social classes; and the political climate created radical parties to fight the status quo.

In the 1930s, Steinbeck also saw the role the natural world played in the lives of men. It was not just economic but also natural forces that sent the American farmer on a trek west, like the pioneers of old, but instead of dreams of gold, the new American dream was of fertile land and a place to call home. Mother Nature, in the form of drought and high winds, drove the farmers from their homes in the Great Plains and beyond, but it was human nature that created the conditions. The group mentality in the early part of the century was to industrialize, tractor up, and expand as much land as possible and plant as many crops as one could. The human drive towards wealth destroyed the land, and nature took care of the rest.

Steinbeck himself fell victim to the "I" versus the "we"—as an individual, he was interested in documenting and writing about the plight of the common man, but his interest in social welfare during the Depression years and beyond led many to brand him a **Communist** agitator and a dangerous radical. The Communist Party (the group) was involved in righting many of the same wrongs that Steinbeck was, but his individual goals were not the same as those of the Party. Regardless, many of his critics did not make that distinction. For them, Steinbeck's "I" was indistinguishable from the "we" they found so threatening.

There was another, more positive element to the "I" and the "we" mentality that emerged in the 1930s. There was a growing sense of community among the downtrodden: a "we" that differed from the "I" of the 1920s. The Roaring Twenties were characterized by an individualistic, self-serving pursuit of wealth and success that was in many ways responsible for the Depression. In their struggles, the ever-increasing number of the nation's poor banded together to form a "we": for the first time, the middle class associated themselves more with working-class poverty than upper-class wealth. The divide between rich and poor was greater than it had ever been, and the sense of community that grew from this divide provided hope in a hopeless time. People would share what little they had with each other. President Roosevelt's New Deal programs sought to provide relief to the struggling citizens. In just a few short years, prosperity had turned to poverty—and a nation and its people were forced to redefine themselves.

In his 1962 Nobel Prize acceptance speech, Steinbeck bemoaned the moral decline he saw in the modern world. Ever a critic of man's destructive nature, he believed that modernity brought with it a level of responsibility: "Having taken Godlike power, we must seek in ourselves for the responsibility and the wisdom we once prayed some deity might have. Man himself has become our greatest hazard and our only hope." Steinbeck took that responsibility very seriously. He was at once a social historian and an artist, seeking "the perfectability of man" in his works of literature. Though he was widely criticized and controversial (his books are among the most frequently banned), Steinbeck never wavered in his attempt to effect change through storytelling—to shift the public consciousness from the "I" to the "we."

Breadlines, such as this one in New York City in 1931, were common throughout the country during the lean years of the Great Depression.

ONE

The Great Depression and the American Farmer

The Great Depression is considered the worst economic crisis in American history. Coming on the heels of the years of prosperity known as the Roaring Twenties, the bleak reality and hardships suffered by many Americans during the 1930s stood in stark contrast to the decadence and wealth of the previous decade. While the Stock Market Crash of 1929 is generally considered to be the starting point of the Great Depression, many causes of the crisis are rooted in American fiscal policy of the 1920s. While economists continue to debate the exact combination of factors that led to the Great Depression, there is no doubt that the Jazz Age boom was in some ways an illusion. Life in rural America was vastly different than life in the industrialized, urban areas—most people did not even have electricity, and the average American farmer was struggling while big business was cashing in.

Panicked citizens gather in the streets outside the New York Stock Exchange on October 31, 1929, two days after the Black Tuesday crash.

The Stock Market Crash

During the boom times of the 1920s, there was no real regulation of the stock market, nor was there very much regulation of bank practices. Although the Federal Reserve (America's central banking system) urged banks not to continue unsafe lending practices and raised interest rates to dissuade them, it had no real power to stop them. The first sign of the market's inevitable decline came in March 1929, and though the market recovered from a mini-crash and panic, in late September and early October prices began to fluctuate. On October 24, stock prices plunged and panic set in. **Margin calls** were issued to investors and 12.9 million shares were traded. Banks and investment companies tried to stop the panic by investing their own money back into the market, and while it briefly stopped people selling stock, it did not last.

October 29, 1929, known as "Black Tuesday," is considered the worst day in the history of the New York Stock Exchange. Prices plummeted, and this time even the banks were desperate to sell. Over sixteen million shares were sold that day. In fact, there was so much activity that the machinery could not keep up with the trading volume and the ticker lagged hours behind. Margin calls were issued, and thousands of investors lost everything. Companies were left in ruins, and the banks were set up for widespread failure.

Bank Failures

With American confidence at a low after the 1929 Wall Street Crash, banks across the nation began to fail. At the time, the banking system in the United States was made up of many smaller local banks and few larger national banks. The Federal Reserve System did not supervise the smaller institutions, and during the 1920s many small, rural banks had already closed their doors. These banks were responsible for lending to farmers, who were left out of the nation's prosperity and often defaulted on their loans. After the crash, panic set in and people began to withdraw money from banks both big and small. Large banks were also responsible for sizeable loans to foreign countries during and after World War I. When the U.S. stopped lending money, European nations defaulted on their loans. The large banks could not meet the withdrawal demands of panicked Americans, who with just a hint that an institution was in trouble, could cause a "run" on a bank, leaving it without sufficient funds. Bank failures affected businesses, local governments, churches, and charity organizations, as well as individuals, since insufficient funds for wages and services contributed to the overall lack of purchasing power.

Decreased Demand and Unemployment

The idea that the Depression left everyone destitute is false, but the panic and anxiety that resulted from the crumbling of America's great financial institutions caused those Americans who did have money to save it instead of spend it. Many Americans stopped buying new clothes, choosing to mend what they already owned, and car sales dropped dramatically as consumers would rather fix an older model than upgrade.

The decrease in consumer demand for goods and services forced companies to decrease production and lay off workers; those who were able to keep their jobs had their hours cut back and their wages lowered. Unemployment rates were highest for African Americans, who were almost always the first to be laid off. As the Depression wore on, it became apparent that no one was immune. White, middle-class Americans, who had bought into the American Dream of upward mobility during the 1920s now found themselves out of work and standing in **breadlines** to feed their families. The wealth gap between the "haves" and the "have nots" was wider than ever before, and for the first time in many years, the middle class identified more with the impoverished lower class.

Hoover's Response

In the wake of the 1929 Crash, President Herbert Hoover attempted to reassure the American people that the economy was sound, stating at a news conference less than a month after the crash that "any lack of confidence in the economic future or basic strength of business in the United States is foolish." Hoover's approach to recovery was to rebuild confidence, but

President Herbert Hoover, who took office only months before the 1929 Stock Market Crash, was blamed by many for the nation's economic troubles.

13

his words did nothing to improve the situation and sounded callous to Americans suffering the effects of the Depression. Hoover was vilified by the public, and the tent communities filled with people who had lost their homes were called "Hoovervilles."

Hoover was not completely inactive, however. He did take action to try and restore the economy, but his philosophy was and had always been that voluntary cooperation between business and government, not government interference in business, was the key to success. Hoover urged industry leaders to maintain high wages so that the people could continue to spend money, but many did not listen. He also encouraged spending through public works projects at the state and local level, but this also failed as those governments quickly ran out of money. The Tariff Act of 1930 (known as the Smoot-Hawley Tariff) was an attempt to restore American business by raising the **tariff** on imported goods so high as to be prohibitive. This approach backfired, as it created hostility between America and countries that relied on trade for the health of their own economies, and these countries stopped purchasing American goods. This was especially harmful to the American farmer, who could no longer rely on income from the export of crops.

Hoover attempted to put an end to the banking crisis through bailouts. While some of his actions were good for business, they did nothing for the growing unemployment rate affecting working-class Americans. The people continued to criticize Hoover for focusing recovery efforts on the institutions they felt were to blame for the Depression. By the time the 1932 presidential election came around, the American people were ready for a change. They had grown hostile toward Hoover and the Republican Party and blamed their inaction and pro-business approach for the worsening Depression. Americans wanted their government to take direct action to help the average person suffering the effects of the economic

Workers in the Civilian Conservation Corps plant laurel in Virginia during one of the CCC's many beautification projects.

crisis, not someone who put business interests first. They found their new leader in the Democratic governor of New York, Franklin Delano Roosevelt.

FDR's First Hundred Days

Roosevelt hit the ground running when he took office in March of 1933, pushing through as many relief programs as he could during the pivotal first hundred days of his presidency in order to combat the worsening Depression. His first action as president was to declare a four-day bank holiday to try to

Franklin Delano Roosevelt (1882–1945)

Democrat Franklin Delano Roosevelt, more commonly known as FDR, took office as the thirty-second president of the United States on March 4, 1933. Born January 30, 1882 in Hyde Park, New York, FDR was a member of the aristocratic Roosevelt family, which included America's twenty-sixth president, Theodore Roosevelt. He had a privileged upbringing and was well educated, but he believed that with privilege came a sense of duty to help the less fortunate. He married his distant cousin, Eleanor Roosevelt, in 1905, and together they began a life of public service. FDR served as a New York state senator (1911-1913), Assistant Secretary to the Navy (1913-1920), and Governor of New York (1929-1932) before being elected president. In 1921, he contracted **polio** and was left paralyzed from the waist down, but he went to great lengths not to show his illness in public. His strength and determination in the face of this debilitating illness is one of the things that endeared him to the American public in their time of hardship.

FDR campaigned on a platform of relief and reform, pledging to take immediate action and promising "a new deal for the American people." He defeated Hoover in a landslide victory and dedicated his first hundred days to sweeping reforms and New Deal programs that would provide immediate relief. While some were more successful than others, FDR remained popular with the American people, who considered him a man of action. His "fireside chats"–evening addresses to the American people broadcast on the radio–brought the president into their living rooms to explain his policies in terms they could understand. His direct communication and cheerful demeanor

gave the American people hope during hard times, and helped him to remain in office despite the fact that he had not managed to bring the country out of the Depression. While the Great Depression only ended as a result of World War II, some of FDR's more successful New Deal programs changed the social, economic, and political landscape of America. After twelve years in office, he died from a massive stroke in Warm Springs, Georgia, on April 12, 1945 during his unprecedented fourth term. FDR remains one of the most beloved and top-rated presidents in the history of the United States.

combat the runs on banks and prevent further institutional failures. He pushed for the passage of the Twenty-First Amendment repealing Prohibition. He passed acts and created government agencies to regulate and improve conditions in industry and agriculture, provide emergency relief funding for American farmers and the growing number of unemployed, and put people to work on public works projects. He also sought to modernize rural America and bring electricity to America's farms, as well as conserve the nation's natural resources.

Roosevelt believed that it was the duty of government to aid the people, but he was conscious of the American attitude toward direct relief. Being "on the dole" (as it was called) was considered shameful by many Americans, especially those men who had always worked for the wages that provided for their families. Early New Deal programs such as the Civilian Conservation Corps (CCC), Civil Works Administration (CWA), Public Works Administration (PWA), and Tennessee Valley Authority (TVA) put Americans to work on projects that would improve and enhance the nation's infrastructure and natural resources, while also improving morale and providing wages to struggling citizens.

The Second New Deal and Reelection

Not all of FDR's early programs were successful, but it was obvious to the American people that their president was actively and aggressively trying to bring the nation out of the Depression. By 1935, the economy was still in trouble, unemployment remained high, and Americans were demanding further action. Roosevelt and the New Deal were receiving criticism from conservatives and liberals alike—the former believing FDR's policies had expanded the role of government too far, and the latter believing they had not done enough for the people.

With criticism pouring in from all sides, FDR launched the Second New Deal in 1935. This wave of reforms was

Louisiana senator Huey Long, an outspoken critic of banks and big business, gives an NBC radio broadcast.

more focused on social welfare and relief than the First New Deal. One of the most important pieces of legislation was the Social Security Act, which established a system of payroll taxes to provide pensions for retirees, as well as unemployment insurance and welfare for the disabled and for families with dependent children. He also greatly expanded his work relief program by creating the Works Progress Administration (WPA), which, in addition to continuing the task of improving

A young woman operates a tractor-driven plow on a farm, circa 1925.

America's infrastructure, provided programs specifically for the arts. One of the boldest new laws was the National Labor Relations Act (or Wagner Act), which legalized trade unions, **collective bargaining,** and striking. It created the National Labor Relations Board (NLRB) to supervise elections in labor unions, investigate unfair labor practices, and resolve disputes between workers and employers.

Despite the fact that America was still in the depths of the Great Depression, FDR was elected for a second term in 1936. His new reform programs and commitment to the welfare of the American people, along with the electorate's hostility toward the pro-business Republican Party, assured his landslide victory over Republican challenger Alfred M. Landon.

The Plight of the American Farmer

Unlike much of the rest of the country, the American farmer did not profit from the boom times of the 1920s, and the agricultural industry was already struggling when the nation entered the Depression. The seeds of the agricultural depression had been sown decades earlier, when the industrialization of American agriculture and "the great plow up" severely damaged the natural resources of the land and set the region up for disaster. The late nineteenth and early twentieth centuries saw westward expansion into the Great Plains region of the United States, where land was cheap but unsuitable for farming. The grasslands of the Plains, while good for grazing livestock, were not suited to planting cash crops, but this did not stop farmers from plowing up acres of land to plant wheat—a staple crop in high demand during World War I. The war years were good to the American farmer, and the U.S. government encouraged Plains farmers to tractor up additional land and overproduce to feed the Allies. Prices were high, and putting more acres into production yielded immediate rewards. However, the plow up removed all the prairie grass, making the **topsoil** vulnerable to the elements.

21

After the war, prices dropped. Farmers were left with a surplus that they could not sell, and more acres in production than were needed. There were also fewer jobs, as industrialization of the industry saw a shift from manual labor and horse- or mule-driven plows to tractors, which enabled farmers to plow more land faster and required fewer workers. The economy of rural America could not sustain its population, but farming was a way of life for many families who chose to stay put and hope for the best. Farmers were left with debt from the loans they had taken out for land and machinery, and the 1920s saw many foreclosures and bank failures in rural areas of the country, which stood in stark contrast to the prosperity elsewhere. There was also a rise in **tenant farming** and **sharecropping**, as many people could no longer afford to own land and were forced to make a living farming acreage owned by others. The financial crisis of the 1930s brought the American farmer even lower, but the crushing blow came from natural, not economic, forces.

The Dust Bowl

Beginning in the early 1930s, the Midwest suffered through drought and a heat wave that killed crops and dried up the topsoil. With the grass plowed up, there was nothing to hold the soil to

A dust storm, or "black blizzard," approaches Springfield, Colorado in May 1937. The storm blocked out the sun for half an hour.

Three women wear masks to keep the dust in the air out of their lungs, circa 1935.

the land, and the high winds of the Plains region created dust storms that left the earth barren. Known as "black blizzards," these storms (which happened with increasing frequency throughout the 1930s) could block out the sun. Livestock choked on the air and died. People sealed their windows and doors with wet rags to try to keep the dust out of their homes, but it got in anyway. They wore masks to keep the dust out of their lungs, but more and more people, especially children, were suffering (and dying) from dust pneumonia as a result of breathing the tainted air. In the 1930s, the Lower Plains (which included areas of Oklahoma, Kansas, Colorado, New Mexico, and Texas) became known as the Dust Bowl.

In addition to the health risks of simply breathing the air, the poverty in the Plains states was widespread. Malnutrition and starvation were common, as families were unable to use the land to grow subsistence crops for the household and did not have enough income to buy all the food they needed. The Agricultural Adjustment Administration (AAA), one of the first New Deal programs, was well-intentioned but actually did more harm than good for many farmers. In theory, taking acreage and livestock out of production would help raise prices, but in practice this did little to help many of the hardest hit. Only the landowners received **subsidies** from the AAA, and by cutting back on production, the AAA program actually put many tenant farmers and sharecroppers out of work. Though this flaw was later corrected so that those who actually worked the land were entitled to government payments, the damage was already done. In addition, the spectacle of destroying crops and livestock while people were starving was a crushing blow to morale in the region. Although proper cultivation and soil conservation techniques were encouraged by the Soil Conservation and Domestic Allotment Act of 1936, the land was already so badly damaged that it would take years to recover.

Migrant Farmers

Even though familial and historical ties to the land were strong, many Dust Bowl farmers decided to pack up their families and head west in search of work. These migrant farmers, known as "Okies" (regardless of whether they hailed from Oklahoma), came in droves to California, where rumors of available jobs and fertile land gave them a glimmer of hope.

California's mild climate made for longer growing seasons and diverse crops. A combination of word-of-mouth information and **handbills** advertising work in the West, which were distributed in hard-hit areas, made California the destination of hundreds of thousands of displaced people from

A homeless family walks on U.S. Highway 99, the major north-south route in California, toward San Diego, where the father hopes to get his family on government relief.

the Lower Plains. Families loaded up as much as they could into cars and trucks and headed west on U.S. Highway 66. Roadside tent communities sprang up along the route where people stopped for rest on the long journey to California's Central Valley. Some men left their families to seek work and ended up riding west in empty train cars, taking only what they could carry. They were known as **bindle stiffs**, named for the bundle of possessions tied to a stick they carried on their journey.

The trip west was difficult, and conditions were not ideal when the migrants arrived. There were more workers than there were jobs. Wages were pitifully low, since employers knew that the mass of unemployed could not afford to turn down a day's pay, however meager. Even if a whole family could find work, the combined wages were not enough to live on. Living conditions were abysmal—tent communities, set up near irrigation ditches in fields, were unsanitary and overcrowded. They were often subject to raids by the local authorities, who (like the rest of the community) were hostile to the "Okies," who they saw as hicks and a drain on their state's resources. There was also fear on the part of the growers' association, Associated Farmers, that these communities would breed radical sentiment and lead workers to unionize and strike.

Government Relief

Two New Deal agencies—the Resettlement Administration (RA) and the Farm Security Administration (FSA)—actively sought to relieve the plight of the displaced American farmer. The RA was formed in 1935 and became the FSA in 1937. Their initial efforts were focused on improving the conditions of migrant laborers. For example, relief camps were built in California to provide a safe and sanitary environment for the growing number of migrant workers pouring into the region. The camps provided clean housing, running water and plumbing, and health services, and they were mostly self-governed. Government administrators allowed camp residents to form committees, a model which minimized the amount of conflict and increased the morale of the migrants, who felt for the first time that they had some level of control over their lives. The experiment was only marginally successful—there was not enough funding to build enough camps to house all those in need, and laborers had to keep moving to go where the work was. There was also a great deal of resistance on the part of the growers to accept the government model for accommodating workers. Those in power believed that the government camps would provide an environment for workers to organize.

World War II and the End of the Depression

Despite the valiant efforts on the part of FDR and the New Dealers, it was World War II that ultimately brought America out of the Depression. Many New Deal programs were decommissioned and money was channeled to the war effort. Even before the U.S. officially entered the war, federal spending and employment were significantly higher than they had been with the New Deal programs. The war created jobs manufacturing weapons and other war supplies, and able-bodied men were drafted into service. Women who did not join the war effort overseas went to work in the factories, providing even more income for families and increasing purchasing power at home.

While the New Deal itself did not bring about the end of the Great Depression, it left a legacy that is still felt today. Social Security and other social welfare programs, federal regulation of banking and the stock market, and many of the labor laws and regulations are all still in place. The nature of federal involvement in industry and relief programs fundamentally changed the relationship between the U.S. government and its citizens.

The Steinbeck House in Salinas, California was the birthplace and childhood home of the author. It is now a restaurant and small museum.

never remember seeing them closed when he awakened. little reflected stars. She was looking at him as she was at him when he awakened.

Kino heard the little splash of morning waves on the beach. Kino closed his eyes again to listen to his music. Perhaps did this and perhaps all of his people did it. His people had

TWO

The Life of John Steinbeck

J ohn Ernst Steinbeck III was born on February 27, 1902 in Salinas, California—the Central California farm town that would become so important to his life and his work. The natural beauty of California at the turn of the century gave young Steinbeck a curiosity and sense of wonder about the natural world, and this curiosity would later extend itself to the people of the region: the laborers who struggled, and average people placed in extraordinary circumstances beyond their control. His respect for the land and its people and the desire for accuracy and authenticity in his work would take its toll on him. He would face harsh criticism from those who were threatened by his realistic portrayal of the people's struggles. He would be ostracized and driven from the land he loved so much. Steinbeck hated being famous—and, to some, infamous—but he refused to compromise to please the critics. He told the stories he felt needed to be told, and for all the problems it brought to his life, his work would place him solidly among the most important American writers of the twentieth century. Much of his fiction and nonfiction leaves behind a painstakingly accurate and realistic description of the American experience during one of the nation's darkest hours: the plight of the American farmer during the Great Depression of the 1930s.

Family Background and Childhood

Both of Steinbeck's parents had roots in the Salinas Valley. His paternal grandfather, John Adolph Grossteinbeck (he later changed his surname to Steinbeck) had come from Germany and moved to a farm near Salinas with his family after the Civil War. His maternal grandfather, Samuel Hamilton, was born in Ireland and settled on a ranch near Salinas with his family. Steinbeck's father grew up working the land but ended up managing a flour mill in King City, where he met his future wife, schoolteacher Olive Hamilton. They married and moved to Salinas, where they started a family.

John Steinbeck was the third of four children (and the only son), and although the Steinbecks were solidly middle class and lived in town, Steinbeck's father kept a garden, raised chickens, and taught his children to ride horses in the countryside. Young Steinbeck also spent time at the Hamilton family ranch and grew up with an appreciation of the land and animals, which he would carry with him for the rest of his life. No matter where he was living, Steinbeck always had a dog.

Steinbeck learned to love the art of storytelling from his mother. She told her children bedtime stories, encouraged them to read, and kept a library in the house. When Steinbeck was young, he enjoyed imaginative stories such as fairy tales and Greek myths, and at age ten he read Sir Thomas Malory's *Le Morte d'Arthur*. This fifteenth-century collection of the legends of King Arthur was the most significant literary influence on young Steinbeck, as it added a love of language to his love of stories. The form and themes of the Arthurian legends would appear in some of his major works, and his last, unfinished project was an attempt to rewrite Malory for the modern world.

Education and Early Work

Steinbeck attended Salinas Valley High, where he served in a cadet program that prepared young men for battle in World War I. More importantly for Steinbeck, the cadets also helped local farmers with their crops during the wartime labor shortage. Steinbeck gained firsthand experience as a farm laborer during high school, working in the bean fields for hours before school. He also took a job digging canals after he graduated, giving him more experience as a laborer.

It was only when Steinbeck entered Stanford University that he began to seriously pursue a literary education. During his time away from Stanford, Steinbeck went back to manual labor. He worked for Spreckels Sugar in various capacities, from harvesting sugar beets to chemical testing to supervising crews of laborers, who were mostly Mexican- and Filipino-Americans. His relationship with the foreign nationals at Spreckels provided him with experience and characters he would use in his work.

Steinbeck took classes at Stanford on and off for six years but never graduated. Though he left in 1925 without a degree, his experience at Stanford had a positive influence on his love of literature, history, and science. Steinbeck would always have an intellectual curiosity and a thirst for all kinds of knowledge.

Steinbeck moved to New York City, where he worked briefly on the construction of Madison Square Garden. He got a job as a newspaper reporter but was soon fired. Steinbeck tried to freelance and write short stories for publication but was unable to find a publisher. He returned to California in 1926 and went to work as a caretaker for the summer home of a wealthy family in Lake Tahoe. For the next two years, Steinbeck worked and wrote in Lake Tahoe. His first professionally published work of fiction, the short story, "The Gifts of Iban," was published in the *Smoker's Companion* in 1927 (under the **pseudonym** John Stern). Isolated and surrounded by nature, his writing efforts intensified during this period, and in 1928 he worked diligently on what would become his first published novel. That same year, Steinbeck went to work at a fish hatchery in Tahoe City. It was there that he met his first wife, Carol Henning.

The Lean Years and the Early Novels

Thanks to his parents' support, Steinbeck was able to concentrate on writing full time. His father allowed him to move into the family beach house in Pacific Grove, California, and gave him an allowance of $25 a month. He continued his relationship with Carol, and in early 1929 he received word that his first novel, *Cup of Gold* (1929), was accepted for publication in August. Steinbeck was not pleased with *Cup of Gold*, a fictionalized tale of the life of Welsh pirate Henry Morgan, but the novel sold fairly well. He received a $250 advance for what he called "the Morgan atrocity," and was able to live comfortably enough to continue writing without having to take on additional work.

John Steinbeck and Carol Henning were married on January 14, 1930 and lived rent-free at the Pacific Grove house. The early 1930s were devastating for the American economy, and Steinbeck himself was not making much of a living from his writing. Carol was a skilled secretary, but like so many others at the time, was unable to find a job. The couple lived on practically nothing, but they made the most of their life together. John and Carol grew their own vegetables in the garden and took advantage of the available seafood in the Pacific. Steinbeck built a fireplace for heat, they used candles for light, and they were comfortable in the cottage with cheap jug wine and the company of friends.

Steinbeck, who disliked being photographed, poses for a picture in the mid-1930s.

Throughout their marriage, Carol was a good editorial influence on Steinbeck. She helped him to refine his style and voice, typed his manuscripts, and corrected his grammar and spelling errors. In the early days of their marriage, Steinbeck was finishing up a novel he had initially called *The Green Lady*, based on a play of the same name written by his Stanford friend, Toby Street. Though it began as a co-authored project, Steinbeck made significant changes to Street's play and completed the project, now titled *To a God Unknown*,

Ed Ricketts

Edward F. Ricketts (1897–1948), known by all as Ed, was a marine biologist who owned a laboratory in Monterey where he collected and preserved specimens for use by schools. Though Ricketts was a scientist, he was also interested in the humanities (having also studied philosophy), and he applied the ecological theories he had observed in Pacific marine life to humans. Steinbeck and Ricketts became fast friends, for Steinbeck had always been interested in animals and nature, and he responded to Ricketts' method of **non-teleological** thinking: that all living

A memorial bust of Ed Ricketts stands in Monterey, California.

creatures behave according to their nature, so there is no "good and evil" or "cause and effect." Most people view the natural world from a **teleological** viewpoint, where they search for a reason or a higher power to explain things, but Ricketts believed that the natural world just *is* and things just happen, and any study of it should focus on the *what* and the *how* instead of the *why*. Ricketts also believed, from

on his own. Unable to find a publisher for the novel, Steinbeck began working on a series of short stories (which would later become *The Pastures of Heaven*), as well as a mystery story called *Murder at Full Moon*. It was around this time, in late 1930, that Steinbeck met Ed Ricketts, a man who would become a lifelong friend and an important influence on his work, as well as his worldview.

In early 1931, Steinbeck's Stanford friend, Ted Miller, who had helped him secure a publisher for his first novel, brought *To a God Unknown* and *Murder at Full Moon* to Mavis McIntosh and Elizabeth Otis of the literary agency McIntosh & Otis. Both women saw great potential in Steinbeck's work, but they could not initially sell either manuscript. McIntosh was particularly interested in *The Pastures of Heaven*, and when Steinbeck completed the manuscript in early 1932, they were able to sell it to Cape and Smith for fall publication. *The Pastures of Heaven* (1932) is the saga of the Munroe family as told through a series of connected short stories, and is the first published example of the influence of non-teleological thinking in Steinbeck's fiction. It is also his first use of the California

his observations of the ecology of coastal Pacific tide pools, that there is a natural order of cooperation and community between various species of organisms and their environment. Many of Ricketts's theories, as applied to human behavior, can be found in Steinbeck's work. Ricketts himself had such a profound influence on Steinbeck that he became the model for many of the characters in his books, most notably Doc in *Cannery Row* and Jim Casy in *The Grapes of Wrath*.

landscape and demonstrates a shift to the more **naturalistic** and descriptive language that characterizes his greatest works. Steinbeck's editor at Cape and Smith, Robert Ballou, had also promised to publish *To a God Unknown*, but the company was experiencing financial difficulties during the early years of the Depression. Ballou eventually published *To a God Unknown* (1933) under his own imprint. This third novel is another early exploration of Steinbeck's themes of the California landscape and of family.

Illness and Success

Olive Steinbeck suffered a massive stroke in early 1933. John and Carol moved into the Steinbeck home in Salinas to help care for her, since Steinbeck's father was not in the best of health himself. Steinbeck hated to be around illness and the stress of caring for his mother was getting to both him and Carol, who shouldered much of the responsibility while John attempted to work. Steinbeck developed one of the great themes of his work—the phalanx theory of man—while he was caring for his dying mother.

Steinbeck equated the way cells make up the human body with the way people make up a society. Each cell has a specific function, and together they make up the body. However, the person is more than just the sum of its cellular components; a person has thoughts, feelings, and goals. In much the same way, events occur in society independent of the thoughts and goals of the individual people. He wrote of this theory to his Stanford friend, Dook Sheffield:

> the group has a soul, a drive, an intent … which in no way resembles the same things possessed by the men who make up the group. These groups have always been considered as individuals multiplied. And they are not so. They are beings in themselves, entities.

Steinbeck's phalanx theory not only applied to his mother's deteriorating body, but also to the deterioration of society during the Depression and during wartime.

In addition to this breakthrough, being home in Salinas inspired Steinbeck to write stories drawn from his childhood memories spent at the Hamilton ranch. Steinbeck's agents sold two of the four stories that would become *The Red Pony* to the *North American Review* for publication in late 1933. The entire collection of stories was later published in the collected volume *The Long Valley* (1938). The most significant work that Steinbeck started during this emotionally draining yet productive time was a draft of his next novel, *Tortilla Flat* (1935), the first of his novels to bring him commercial success and recognition.

Shortly after his mother's death in February of 1934, Steinbeck completed the manuscript. Around the same time, an editor named Pascal "Pat" Covici of Covici-Friede was given copies of *Cup of Gold* and *The Pastures of Heaven*. Covici saw extraordinary potential in Steinbeck and contacted him through his agents. He not only wanted to publish *Tortilla Flat* but also to reissue Steinbeck's other novels. Covici would remain Steinbeck's publisher and friend for the next thirty years until his death in 1964.

Tortilla Flat was Steinbeck's first successful novel. It is the story of a group of **paisanos** (people of mixed Spanish, Indian, Mexican, and Caucasian descent) living in a poor area outside Monterey (called Tortilla Flat). The paisanos are based on real-life individuals with whom Steinbeck was familiar, both from his own experiences with the Mexican Americans he worked with at Spreckels and from stories he had heard from a friend. This episodic novel of connecting stories incorporates aspects of the Arthurian legends, further explores the California landscape, and demonstrates Steinbeck's growing interest in

Mexican laborers work on a sugar beet farm near Stockton, California.

realistic depictions of the common man's struggles in society. Written during the height of the Depression, the novel is an exploration of how money and property ownership can destroy the sense of community and friendship among men. *Tortilla Flat* was a financial success (Paramount Pictures bought the film rights soon after its release) and with it came the fame that would make Steinbeck increasingly uncomfortable over the years.

The Dust Bowl Trilogy

Steinbeck became aware of the growing problems in California, especially the conditions of the Dust Bowl migrants and the increase in labor strife between union workers and growers. *In Dubious Battle* (1936) was the first of his "Dust Bowl Trilogy" (also known as the "California Trilogy") and focused on the labor problem. Since 1932, the Communist Party had had a major influence on labor organization in the region, and Steinbeck met a number of labor organizers and supporters when he and Carol returned to Pacific Grove. While Steinbeck sympathized with many Communist causes, he himself was never a Communist. He was, however, very interested in hearing the stories and experiences of strikers. *In Dubious Battle* is the story of a fictionalized strike, based mostly on the San Joaquin Valley cotton pickers' strike of October 1933 and incorporating elements of the Tagus Ranch peach strike of August 1933. The novel explores Steinbeck's phalanx theory as it applies to individuals and members of the opposing organizations: the Party and the growers. *In Dubious Battle* was well reviewed but controversial in its subject matter, and Steinbeck was branded a radical and a suspected Communist—false accusations that would only get worse with subsequent works.

Crowds gather in the street during an oil workers' strike, circa 1930.

FSA administrator Tom Collins speaks with a resident of the Kern migrant worker camp in Kern County, California.

Steinbeck's next novels also took inspiration from current events, though the focus shifted from labor unions to the plight of the California migrant farmers. For *Of Mice and Men* (1937), which Steinbeck began writing in early 1936, the author drew from his own experiences as a laborer. Though his employment took place before the influx of Dust Bowl migrants, Steinbeck used his firsthand knowledge of the land and the people to craft the story of two bindle stiffs searching for work and a home to call their own during the Depression years. While Steinbeck was completing *Of Mice and Men*, he was contacted by George West of the *San Francisco News*. West had read *In Dubious Battle* and wanted Steinbeck to write a series of articles for the paper about California's migrant farmers.

During the summer of 1936, Steinbeck hit the road in "the pie wagon"—a bakery truck he had converted into a camper—and visited the California migrant camps. At this time, the New Deal Resettlement Administration (RA) was in the process of establishing government camps for California's migrant population, and the RA assigned camp manager Tom Collins to accompany Steinbeck on his tour of the region. Collins was working at the Weedpatch camp in Arvin at the time, and he provided Steinbeck with firsthand experience as well as copies of his detailed reports on camp conditions. Collins's reports document the lives of the people in the camps and the migrant culture, including dialect and anecdotes. These reports, as well as Steinbeck's personal experiences, provided the author with the inspiration and material for the last novel in his Dust Bowl Trilogy, *The Grapes of Wrath* (1939).

After writing his series of seven articles for the *News*, collectively called "The Harvest Gypsies" (October 5–12, 1936), Steinbeck went to work on what he called his "big book." His first attempt resulted in a more satirical, propaganda-based version called "L'Affaire Lettuceberg," but he decided to abandon that in favor of a more artistic long novel. He wrote *The Grapes of Wrath* between May and December 1938 and completed it at a punishing pace, sacrificing his health in the process. The novel was published in 1939 and became one of the great American novels of the twentieth century. *The Grapes of Wrath* won Steinbeck the Pulitzer Prize in 1940, but fame and success brought Steinbeck trouble.

The Price of Fame

The success and recognition after the publication of *The Grapes of Wrath* reinforced everything that Steinbeck feared about fame. He was physically and mentally exhausted, he was accused of creating Communist propaganda by politicians and the growers' corporations, and his marriage was crumbling. Carol had been invaluable to Steinbeck during the writing of the novel, typing his manuscript and managing everything so he could focus (and it is dedicated, in part, "To CAROL who willed it"), but their marriage was in shambles.

Relations between John and Carol were strained when the two went on an expedition trip with Ed Ricketts down the coast to Baja, California, to study marine life. In addition to wanting to escape the public scrutiny he faced after his last novel, Steinbeck was tired of writing fiction and decided to focus on his interest in ecology. Out of this trip came *The Log from the Sea of Cortez* (1951). This was a revised portion from the travelogue, *Sea of Cortez* (1941), that Ricketts and Steinbeck co-authored when they returned from their trip. The trip did nothing to improve relations between John and Carol and they spent most of their time together arguing. The strain of writing *The Grapes of Wrath* and the beginning of Steinbeck's relationship with his second wife, Gwyn Conger, caused John and Carol Steinbeck to separate in 1941. Toward the end of his marriage, Steinbeck spent much of his time in Hollywood where *Of Mice and Men* was in production and *The Grapes of Wrath* was in development, and more and more of it had been spent with Gwyn. His divorce from Carol was finalized in 1943, and shortly after he wed Gwyn.

The War Years

The early 1940s saw America back at war. Before the United States entered World War II after the bombing of a naval base in Pearl Harbor, Hawaii, on December 7, 1941, Steinbeck had been working as a war correspondent for the Foreign Information Service (FIS) and formulated the idea for a political play/novel, *The Moon is Down* (1942). The novel, originally set in enemy-occupied America, brought some criticism from the FIS, who felt that it would hurt morale. Steinbeck then changed the setting to an unnamed Nazi-occupied country (most closely associated with Norway); the novel resonated with foreign resistance movements and was illegally distributed through underground channels in occupied European nations. It sold well in America, despite the critics, and opened as a play a few months after publication. Better reviewed was the nonfiction war propaganda piece, *Bombs Away* (1942), which Steinbeck wrote for the U.S. Air Force after spending time on base with American bomber crews around the nation.

In the early days of his marriage to Gwyn in 1943, Steinbeck travelled back to the front lines in Europe and North Africa as a correspondent for the *New York Herald Tribune*. After touring with the troops and witnessing the horrors of war, he returned to the U.S. and went back to fiction with his next book, *Cannery Row* (1945). It was a light novel, set in the real-life Cannery Row area of Monterey, which contained the fish processing plants. In addition to the biologist Doc, based on Ed Ricketts, the novel hosts a cast of characters that includes bums, prostitutes, and other outcasts of Monterey society. Though comedic, the novel contains aspects from *Sea of Cortez* and presents Steinbeck's non-teleological viewpoint, and beneath the comedy Steinbeck presents the theme of decaying American values.

Steinbeck took a break from writing *Cannery Row* to travel to Mexico with Gwyn, where he began plotting a screenplay for a film based on a folk tale in *Sea of Cortez*. The screenplay and the original short story, "The Pearl of the World" (1945), would later become a short novel, *The Pearl* (1947). Like *Cannery Row*, the story of *The Pearl* demonstrates Steinbeck's growing disillusionment with the American pursuit of wealth (as his own success continued to bring him trouble).

The Cannery Row area of Monterey, California was memorialized in Steinbeck's novel of the same name.

Steinbeck and Gwyn returned from Mexico and in August 1944, Gwyn gave birth to their first child, Thomas "Thom" Steinbeck. After a brief time spent in Monterey, Steinbeck returned to Mexico to work on the film version of *The Pearl*. When he returned, he and a pregnant Gwyn moved back to New York. Their second son, John IV, was born in June 1946, but by that time Steinbeck's marriage to Gwyn was already starting to fall apart.

Despite the distraction of two small children and tension with Gwyn disrupting his work, Steinbeck managed to write the manuscript for his next novel, *The Wayward Bus* (1947). Gwyn was jealous of her husband's fame, and tensions between the two grew during a 1946 trip to Europe when Steinbeck was awarded the King Haakon Liberty Cross in Norway for *The Moon is Down*, which was very popular with the resistance movement there. A trip to the Soviet Union, accompanied by photographer Robert Capa, resulted in *A Russian Journal* (1948), Steinbeck's travelogue of his experiences with the common people living under Stalin during the early years of the Cold War.

Endings and New Beginnings

Steinbeck suffered two major losses in 1948: Ed Ricketts died in a car accident in May, and just days later, Gwyn asked for a divorce. Gwyn took the children to California, refusing to allow Steinbeck any contact. When their divorce was finalized in October, Gwyn returned to their New York apartment, and would not allow Steinbeck access to the writing materials he had left there. Steinbeck moved back to Pacific Grove briefly, where he suffered a bout of depression, and spent time in Mexico working on the screenplay for *Viva Zapata!* (1952), a film based on the life of Mexican revolutionary leader Emiliano Zapata.

Steinbeck stands with his third wife, Elaine, as she takes a photograph in Rome, Italy in 1952.

Steinbeck met his third wife, Elaine Scott, in May 1949. Though Elaine was still married at the time, she was on her way to divorce, and her relationship with Steinbeck continued to blossom as he finished up work on *Viva Zapata!* and moved on to his next play/novel, *Burning Bright* (1950). His most important project in the years following Ricketts's death and his divorce from Gwyn was another long novel that he was calling "The Salinas Valley," but which he would publish as *East of Eden* (1952). This highly personal novel, set in Steinbeck's home county, tells the story of the Trask and Hamilton families and, uncharacteristically, Steinbeck used stories from his own ancestors (his mother's side of the family, the Hamiltons). While the novel was not completely autobiographical (the story of the Trask family is based on the Biblical story of Cain and Abel) it was a departure from Steinbeck's usual brand of social realism and included more of the author in the narrative than his previous works. *East of Eden* was a critical and commercial success. *Sweet Thursday* (1954), a sequel to *Cannery Row*, was not so successful, and it failed both as a novel and as a play (the theatrical version was called *Pipe Dreams*).

The Later Years

Steinbeck was a New Deal Democrat and in his later years he covered the Democratic and Republican conventions for the *Louisville Courier-Journal* as well as wrote campaign speeches for Adlai Stevenson. He also volunteered to work in President Dwight D. Eisenhower's cultural exchange program, People to People, which brought together citizens from the U.S. and the Soviet Union during the Cold War.

After the publication of an unsuccessful novel, *The Short Reign of Pippin IV* (1957), Steinbeck focused on writing an Arthurian book, which he researched in England off and on but never completed. In 1960 he stopped work on the Arthurian novel to work on *The Winter of Our Discontent* (1961), a

Steinbeck (third from the right) stands with the other Nobel Prize winners at the banquet in Stockholm, Sweden on December 10, 1962.

story influenced by his concern for what he saw as America's declining morality. Steinbeck felt he was losing touch with his country and set off to travel around the U.S. with his dog, Charley, in a camper called "Rocinante." His experiences on his trip would become *Travels With Charley in Search of America* (1962).

In 1962, Steinbeck won the Nobel Prize for Literature, which brought a lot of criticism from people who felt he had not written anything of merit since *The Grapes of Wrath* and the usual derision from those who viewed him as a radical. In his Nobel acceptance speech, he summed up his view of a writer's purpose, declaring that the writer in the modern world "is charged with exposing our many grievous faults and failures, with dredging up to the light our dark and dangerous dreams for the purpose of improvement." Steinbeck's failing health, and the critical response to his Nobel Prize, took a toll on him and he was unable to complete a novel. The deaths of Pat Covici in late 1964 and his sister Mary soon after contributed to his inability to write. A series of essays about America, completed in early 1964, would become his last book published during his lifetime, *America and Americans* (1966).

At the personal request of President John F. Kennedy, Steinbeck took another cultural exchange trip in 1963, touring Eastern Europe and the Soviet Union with Elaine. After Kennedy's assassination, Steinbeck became friends with his successor, Lyndon B. Johnson, and helped write speeches for his 1964 campaign. In 1966–1967, the Steinbecks traveled to Vietnam, where the U.S. Army (including Steinbeck's son John IV) was fighting the Viet Cong. Steinbeck worked as a war correspondent for a Long Island newspaper, *Newsday*, but true to form, his articles focused on the human aspect of war—the soldiers—and did not politicize the conflict.

Steinbeck's health was quite poor upon his return from Vietnam and he required back surgery, from which he never fully recovered. The arrest of his son John IV for marijuana possession brought unwanted attention at a time when he should have been recuperating, and he never wrote for publication again. On December 20, 1968, with Elaine at his side, John Ernst Steinbeck fell into a coma and died in his New York City apartment. He was laid to rest in Salinas with his parents and his sister.

John

STEINBECK

Of Mice and Men

THREE

Of Mice and Men

O f *Mice and Men* was published in February of 1937 and was an instant success, both critically and commercially. The **novella** was chosen as a Book of the Month Club selection and sold 117,000 advance copies. During the writing process, Steinbeck experimented with the novel form, and he wrote *Of Mice and Men* with a theatrical production in mind. The book became the first of many play/novelettes he would write. The first stage production of *Of Mice and Men* opened on Broadway in November 1937. A film adaptation followed in 1939—the first of many movie and television versions that would be created over the years. Although it is one of the most studied works of Steinbeck's fiction, *Of Mice and Men* remains controversial for its use of profanity and is on the list of most frequently banned books in America.

Plot Summary

Of Mice and Men is the story of George Milton and Lennie Small, two bindle stiffs in Depression-era California who

A view of a pond in the fertile Salinas Valley where *Of Mice and Men* takes place.

dream of owning a little piece of land they can call their own. They travel from ranch to ranch, looking for work and trying to save up enough so they can make a life for themselves, but the harsh realities of the world they live in make their dream impossible.

The novel opens with George and Lennie stopping by a riverbank in the Salinas Valley on their way to their next job. The two men travel together, with George looking after Lennie, who is mentally disabled. George has taken on the responsibility of caring for Lennie, who is large and unaware of his own physical strength. Lennie, who often does not understand the world around him and needs George to repeat things, is driven by simple, sensory pleasures like the taste of ketchup and petting soft animals. His desire to touch soft things combined with his strength and lack of understanding tends to get him into trouble, as evidenced by the dead mouse he carries in his pocket.

The two men settle in to spend the night by the river and George bemoans the fact that he could "live so easy" without Lennie, but the life he describes is a lonely one, typical of many of the itinerant men looking for work at the time. He reprimands Lennie for his actions at their last job in Weed, where he had grabbed a woman's dress to "pet it like it was a mouse" and frightened her, losing them their jobs and forcing them to make a run for it. Though George is giving Lennie a hard time about it, the way he relates to him is paternal, and when he sees Lennie's "anguished face" he stops berating him.

Lennie wants George to tell him "about the rabbits," a story George has clearly told many times before. George tells Lennie that most men are lonely, but that they are different because they have each other. This gives them hope for the future, when they can own a small house and a farm together and "live off the fatta the lan'." They will keep rabbits on the farm and Lennie will be allowed to tend to them, and it is obvious that the rabbits are the most important thing to him. Lennie does not understand the larger significance of land ownership as George does.

George reminds Lennie of his earlier instructions: Lennie is not to speak if the ranch boss asks him questions. George knows that Lennie's disability makes him undesirable to an employer, even though his physical strength makes him a superior worker. George also tells Lennie that if he gets into trouble again, he is to return to the spot by the pool, hide, and wait. It is a given that George, his protector, will come for him.

African American migrant workers are lodged in a barn turned bunkhouse while they work as fruit pickers in Michigan, July 1940.

The next day George and Lennie arrive at the ranch. They are shown to the **bunkhouse** by an older man named Candy, who is missing a hand. Candy tells them that the ranch boss was not happy that they arrived late. Soon the boss himself, who is not named in the novel, arrives wearing "high-heeled boots and spurs to prove he was not a laboring man." As discussed, George speaks for Lennie and the boss grows suspicious of them. The boss's first instinct is to accuse George of taking advantage of Lennie because he cannot understand that he would travel with another man without an ulterior motive. George lies and tells the boss that Lennie is his cousin who was kicked in the head by a horse as a child, and that he promised to look after him. While the details of the story are not accurate, as Lennie later points out, the nature of their relationship is no different: George does look out for Lennie, who is unable to look after himself.

Not long after, the boss's son, Curley, enters the bunkhouse. Curley is presented as a small man, and when he sees George and Lennie he takes an aggressive stance. Like his father, Curley questions the nature of the relationship between George and Lennie, forcing Lennie to talk against his will. Once Curley leaves, Candy tells them that Curley is "like a lot of little guys" and constantly picks fights with larger men, "like he's mad at 'em because he ain't a big guy." Curley is insecure, but his position as the son of the ranch owner allows him to act without repercussions. George is immediately wary of him: since Lennie "don't know no rules," George is concerned that he will hurt Curley if he is provoked. George tells a frightened Lennie to stay away from Curley. As before, he makes him repeat what he is supposed to do if there is trouble.

Another form of trouble, Curley's unnamed wife, enters the bunkhouse. Candy had previously told George that she flirts with the men on the ranch, and when she enters it becomes obvious to George that she is "jail bait." Lennie thinks she's "purty," but George quickly tells him to keep away from her. Though Lennie does not understand why, he has a bad feeling about the ranch and tells George that he wants to leave, but George knows that they need the work in order to save money for their dream. He tells Lennie they have to stick it out until the job is done.

A man named Slim enters the bunkhouse. He is presented as "the prince of the ranch" although he is also a worker. He is the lead mule driver and respected by all the men. He has a

This 1935 photograph by Walker Evans, entitled *Young Boy*, depicts one of the nation's many homeless teenage boys on the road searching for work during the Depression years.

quiet authority about him, in contrast to Curley's aggressive leadership, that was "so great that his word was taken on any subject." Slim is friendly to George and Lennie and while he, too, questions their traveling together, he is the first person who seems to understand and accept it. Despite his being understanding and friendly, Slim also knows that certain things must be done for survival. For example, when Carlson enters and inquires about the litter of pups Slim's dog just birthed, Slim tells him he drowned four of them because the litter was too large. Just before the dinner bell rings, Carlson suggests that they kill Candy's old, lame dog and replace it with one of the pups from the litter.

Slim and George return to the bunkhouse after a day's work. Slim has given Lennie one of the puppies, and he is out in the barn with it. George thanks him for that kindness and proceeds to open up to Slim about their relationship, since he is the only one at the ranch that George feels comfortable talking to. George admits to having initially taken advantage of Lennie's disability, mocking him and telling him to do things because he knew Lennie would do whatever he said, but that he stopped after an incident where he put Lennie in danger. Slim can see that Lennie is a gentle person, and he points out to George, "Guy don't need no sense to be a nice fella … Take a real smart guy and he ain't hardly ever a nice fella." George then tells Slim the story of the incident in Weed, and Slim understands that Lennie is "jes' like a kid."

The rest of the men enter and Carlson, who can't stand the smell of Candy's dog, tries to convince Candy to let him shoot it. Candy, who has had the dog since he was a pup, is understandably resistant. Slim agrees that the dog should be shot, and offers him a pup from the litter as a replacement. Unlike Carlson, who only sees that the dog is useless in its old age, Slim says that Candy's dog "ain't no good to himself" and should be put out of its misery. With the promise that the dog will be shot in the back of the head and killed quickly and humanely, Candy finally agrees, and Carlson takes the dog outside and shoots it. Candy later regrets not having done it himself.

George plays cards with a man named Whit, who tells him about the local houses of prostitution, but George is uninterested in spending his wages on alcohol and women like the other men do. He does not seek immediate gratification for himself but works toward his shared goal of the farm. There are rumors of a potential fight between Slim and Curley in the barn, and all the men go out to watch, leaving George, Lennie, and Candy behind. George again warns Lennie about Curley's wife, but Lennie just wants to hear the story of the farm again.

George tells him it will be a place where they would belong with "no more runnin' round the country."

Candy overhears them talking. He wants to be a part of their dream, and offers what money he has to help them buy a place. Candy knows that before long, he won't be of any use on the ranch and will be put out with no place to go. George is hesitant, but the reality of having enough money to make it happen makes the dream seem within reach for the first time: "This thing they had never really believed in was coming true."

This hope soon begins to dwindle as the other men come back. Curley, all riled up and looking for a fight, sees Lennie smiling about the farm and assumes he is laughing at him. A fight ensues in which Lennie, frightened by Curley's attack and given permission from George to fight back, breaks Curley's hand. Slim, knowing the incident was not Lennie's fault, tells Curley to lie about the source of his injury lest he be mocked and humiliated—the thing an insecure man like Curley fears most. Lennie is only afraid that he won't get to tend the rabbits.

On Saturday night, all the men go into town, leaving only Lennie, Candy, and Crooks (the African American **stable buck**). Lennie stumbles upon Crooks's room when he goes to see his puppy in the barn. Initially, Crooks tells him to leave. As a black man, Crooks is not allowed in the bunkhouse and doesn't want Lennie, a white man, in his space. Lennie does not understand the concept of race, however, and Crooks allows him to come in and talk.

Forgetting his promise to George, Lennie talks about the farm. Crooks is cruel to him, and scares him into thinking that George is not coming back for him. He stops when Lennie starts to get visibly upset and tells Lennie, "a guy goes nuts if he ain't got nobody." As a black man, Crooks is completely isolated on the ranch, and he understands better than anyone what loneliness can do. He puts down Lennie's dream, telling him that he has seen hundreds of men come through with the

About the Author

Alison Morretta holds a Bachelor of Arts in English and Creative Writing from Kenyon College in Gambier, Ohio, where she studied the history and literature of the Great Depression. She has worked in book publishing since 2005, developing and copy editing both fiction and nonfiction manuscripts. Alison lives in New York City with her loving husband, Bart, and their rambunctious Corgi, Cassidy. In addition to this title, Alison has penned two other books in this series, *F. Scott Fitzgerald and the Jazz Age* and *Harriet Beecher Stowe and the Abolitionist Movement*.

same dream of a piece of land to call their own and that none of them ever get it. When Candy comes in, Crooks learns that they have most of the money they need, and he allows himself for a moment to dream of being a part of it. However, the men are soon interrupted by Curley's wife.

Curley's wife is lonely and unhappy, but the men are not sympathetic. They view her only as a threat and they want her to leave. When Crooks tells her she doesn't belong there, she threatens him with lynching and he "reduce[s] himself to nothing … no personality, no ego—nothing to arouse either like or dislike." He knows that he is powerless to change his fate.

The next day, while the other men play horseshoes, Lennie is alone in the barn. He has accidentally killed his puppy as he did with the mouse, but he does not understand why creatures keep dying when he does not mean to kill them. He tries to hide the puppy so George doesn't find out, and soon Curley's wife comes into the barn. When she talks to Lennie about her life, she is presented for the first time as a sympathetic character. As a woman on the ranch, she is also suffering from isolation. She, too, had a dream—to become a movie star—but she did not achieve it and has ended up alone, married to a man she hates. Lennie tells her about the rabbits and that he likes to pet nice things, and Curley's wife offers him her hair. As when he touched the dress of the woman in Weed, Lennie's strength frightens Curley's wife. She struggles to get away, and in the process Lennie snaps her neck.

To Lennie, Curley's wife's death is no different from the puppy's: he did not mean to do it, and he is only concerned with the threat it might pose to his future of tending the rabbits. As he did with the puppy, Lennie tries to cover Curley's wife with hay. Realizing he is in trouble again, Lennie remembers George's instructions and flees to the woods. When Candy and George discover what has happened, George knows that their dream is over, telling Candy that he "knowed we'd

never do her" but that Lennie "usta like to hear about it so much I got to thinking maybe we would." George asks Candy to wait to tell the other men so that he isn't a suspect, and Candy obliges.

When the men reach the barn, they all suspect Lennie, and Curley insists that they go after him. George, who pretends not to know anything, goes with them. Slim is again the voice of reason, and he tells George that Lennie is better off dead than dying at the hands of a lynch mob or locked up in jail. George knows what he has to do, and he goes off to look for Lennie by the river, where he knows he will be waiting.

A frightened Lennie has lost what ability to reason he had. He begins to hallucinate, seeing first his Aunt Clara and then a giant rabbit, each reprimanding him for what he has done. George soon appears and comforts him by going through the motions of scolding him as Lennie expects him to and then telling him the story of their dream. He makes Lennie turn away from him and remove his hat, and as he finishes the story of their dream for the last time, he shoots Lennie in the back of the head. Slim, Carlson, and Curley arrive, and George tells them that Lennie had the gun. Only Slim knows the truth and understands. He consoles George, telling him that he had no choice. The novel ends with Curley and Carlson confused as to why the other two men are upset.

Cultural Context

Of Mice and Men is the second of Steinbeck's "Dust Bowl Trilogy" of the late 1930s, in which he explores the contemporary problems of laborers in California after the influx of migrants from the East. The Depression years were devastating for the average American farmer, especially in the Great Plains region where high winds and drought conditions made the land unsuitable for living or farming. Many people lost everything they had and uprooted their lives and families

Mexican American workers, often favored by growers who assumed they would tolerate low pay and poor living conditions, wait for a ride to the melon fields in Imperial Valley, California, June 1935.

to seek work and a better life in California. Life in the West was not what the migrants expected: work was scarce and wages were low due to the surplus of available laborers. There was no place to settle down as workers had to move with the harvest, and the people of California, especially the upper class growers who owned the farms, were hostile to the migrants.

Steinbeck drew from his own experiences for this novel, using his time as a laborer to realistically replicate the landscape and the bunkhouse. The ranch in the novel is based on the

ranches in the Salinas Valley owned by Spreckels Sugar, where Steinbeck worked as a young man. Though his own experiences took place before the influx of Dust Bowl migrants, Steinbeck used his knowledge of the land and its people to tell the story of two bindle stiffs trying to "get the jack together" to buy a place where they can "live off the fatta the lan'."

Major Characters

George Milton

George is a migrant farmer with a dream of owning his own small property. He looks after his friend, Lennie, who is mentally disabled and shares this dream with him. George is the only character in the novel that has any development. Although he complains about Lennie and used to take advantage of him, George came to realize that it was morally wrong to exploit Lennie's weakness. He is very paternal and responsible in the way he protects Lennie, and his commitment to his friend is something that many other people do not understand. His dream of the farm is also a dream of a place where he and Lennie can be safe. Though he does everything in his power to protect Lennie, he cannot change the world around them, where the strong prey on the weak and the weak prey on the weaker. George's dream dies when he realizes that the best thing he can do for Lennie is to kill him humanely, and that he is destined to live a solitary life.

Lennie Small

Lennie is a mentally disabled yet physically strong man. He has the mind of a child and the instinctive responses of an animal, but he does not have the ability to reason. Steinbeck compares Lennie to a bear and a horse, but in his loyalty to George, he is much like a dog. Lennie relies on George, who keeps him safe and tells him what he is supposed to do, but Lennie

often forgets or finds himself in situations he cannot control. Lennie shares George's dream of the farm, but to Lennie the most important thing about the farm is the rabbits he will keep. Lennie gets pleasure out of sensory experiences, such as petting soft things, and in his inability to understand the world, he truly believes that he and George will get their farm one day because George says they will. Lennie does not develop at all throughout the novel—from the beginning to the end he looks at the world very simply and blindly follows George's instructions—and he serves more to bring out the character traits of those around him. The way people in the novel react to Lennie says a great deal about what kind of people they are. Lennie is kind but completely helpless, which seals his fate in the harsh world of the migrant worker.

Major Themes

Friendship and Community

George and Lennie are unique among the rest of the ranch workers because they travel together. Lennie needs George to help him survive, but George also needs Lennie's companionship to keep him human. Without Lennie, George would have no responsibilities. He would spend his money on vices, and never even dream of saving and settling down. While many characters in the novel do not comprehend their companionship and assume that George must be taking advantage of Lennie in some way, some of the men understand the dangers of a lonely life. Crooks, who is the most isolated of all the novel's characters because he is black, understands this better than most, telling Lennie that "a guy goes nuts if he ain't got nobody … a guy gets too lonely an' he gets sick."

The closest that any of the characters come to happiness is when the dream of buying the farm starts to become a

possibility. Candy, who has just lost his only companion (his dog), offers to give George all his savings if he can join them. Even Crooks, though he knows that every bindle stiff that passes through the ranch has the same fantasy, briefly allows himself to dream that he might go with them. This is an early example of Steinbeck's phalanx theory—the transition from the "I" to the "we"—in which changes occur when individuals join a group. In this case, the group is made up of the novel's dispossessed, and the dream of the farm only seems possible as a group effort. The group mentality also allows connections to form despite the superficial differences (race, age, handicap) between the men, as they all share one common goal of a better life, and that life is only achievable if they are in it together.

The Failure of the American Dream

Where the American Dream of the 1920s was an individualistic pursuit of wealth and excess, the new American Dream of the 1930s was to have security and the most basic of human necessities—just enough land for a roof over one's head and a farm to sustain one's self, a place where one belonged and had control, a place to feel safe. This was all but impossible for the vast majority of Americans during the Depression, and especially so for African Americans and women. The opportunities for employment were few, and what jobs there were generally went to white men.

The life of a migrant worker without a family was a solitary existence, and a hard enough life if you were a healthy, white male like George. Any disadvantage, be it mental, physical, or racial, made life much more difficult. The characters in the novel represent different kinds of disabilities that society viewed as weakness: Lennie is mentally disabled, Candy is physically disabled and aging, Crooks is black, and Curley's wife is the lone woman in the man's world of the ranch. All these characters have a certain dispossession and hopelessness

African American migrant workers wait in line for relief in the form of surplus goods in Belle Glade, Florida. African Americans were generally the first fired and the last hired during the Depression years.

about their lives, but Lennie is the only one who does not understand that. What they knew, and Lennie did not grasp, is that the life of a migrant farmer was driven, above all else, by the need to survive, and many things outside a person's control put them at a disadvantage.

Part of George's dream is about community and helping others—that "if a fren' come along, why we'd have an extra bunk." As Slim put it, it seemed as if "ever'body in the whole

damn world is scared of each other," and part of George's vision of a better life is to create a place of kindness and generosity, so absent in a world where a starving man is underpaid to harvest food he cannot eat. Steinbeck presents the failure of the American Dream in the context of the Depression, when economic, social, and natural forces guided people's lives. The will and desire of men to work hard to achieve a goal was no longer enough to ensure a comfortable, happy life, and the tragedy of the story is that man cannot change his environment: the structure of society puts the migrant farmers at a disadvantage they cannot possibly overcome. In George and Lennie's world, there is no place for disability and weakness and, as in nature, only the fittest survive. While a sense of community can give hope to the dispossessed, their reality is grim and unchangeable and their dream ultimately impossible.

Major Symbol: Animals

Steinbeck's working title for the novel was "Something That Happened," and this is applicable in the **deterministic** way he presents the events of the story: the characters have very little to no control over what happens to them. There is a natural order of things in the animal world, and the world of man is no different. Steinbeck's scientific approach to nature comes through in his descriptive passages about the Salinas Valley landscape and the animals that inhabit it. However, he also uses nature to demonstrate how man is just a different kind of animal. At the idyllic pool by the river, Steinbeck presents a heron stalking its prey, and describes very matter-of-factly how the heron swallows a snake alive. The scene is presented in a naturalistic style, but in juxtaposing it with Lennie's imminent death, Steinbeck suggests that in the life of man there are also predators and prey.

Throughout the novel, Lennie is described in animalistic terms—his hand is like a "big paw," and he drinks from the

pool like a horse. Because Lennie is unable to reason, he is closer to an animal than to a man. While Lennie is technically responsible for injuring Curley and killing Curley's wife, these events are all presented as things that just happened (like his accidental killings of the mice and the puppy). There was no intent to harm on Lennie's part. While mentally challenged, he is physically stronger than anyone else in the novel and when he is frightened, his survival instincts kick in and result in tragedy. Just as one would not consider the heron eating the snake to be murder, Lennie's killings are presented as natural responses to his environment.

The most important animal imagery in the novel is that of Candy's old dog. Like Lennie's relationship to George, Candy's dog was his companion, but it had lived past its use and the other men believed it should be killed. Candy allowed Carlson to shoot his dog and regretted not doing it himself. In comparison, once George realizes that Lennie will be made to suffer if he is killed by Curley's mob, he knows that he has to shoot Lennie himself. Like Candy's dog, Lennie is considered useless by the rest of the men, and he is killed in the exact same manner. Only the characters who understand the importance of companionship (George, Slim, and Candy) are saddened by Lennie's death. To the others, he is no more than a lame animal to be put down.

STEINBECK
THE GRAPES
OF WRATH
COMPLETE AND UNABRIDGED

THE GRAPES OF WRATH JOHN STEINBECK

A BANTAM BOOK

PATHFINDER NOVEL

FOUR

The Grapes of Wrath

P ublished by Viking Press in April 1939, *The Grapes of Wrath* was an immediate success and had sold one million copies by 1941. The novel was considered controversial by many critics and readers, especially the California officials and members of the Associated Farmers, and branded a work of Communist propaganda, but Steinbeck was thorough in his research for the book. Along with government administrator Tom Collins, Steinbeck visited both roadside Hoovervilles and Weedpatch, the government-run camp at Arvin. Using his own experiences, as well as Collins's meticulous reports, Steinbeck had a wealth of material to work from when crafting his novel about the Dust Bowl migration to California.

He was deeply affected by what he saw during his visits to the migrant camps and horrified by labor strikes in the region that had turned violent. This hit close to home in the case of the Salinas Lettuce Strike of 1936. Steinbeck went through a number of versions of the story, one of which was "L'Affaire Lettuceberg," a scathing satirical response to the injustices of

A farmer and his sons walk past a half-buried building during a dust storm in Cimarron County, Oklahoma, April 1936.

Depression-era America. Ultimately, he abandoned it in favor of a more artistic, literary approach. *The Grapes of Wrath* won Steinbeck a Pulitzer Prize and was quickly made into a film, directed by John Ford, which debuted in 1940.

Plot Summary

The Grapes of Wrath is both the tale of the Joads, an Oklahoma farm family fleeing the Dust Bowl for California, and a more universal story about the plight of the poor in America during the Great Depression. Steinbeck accomplishes this in the structure of the novel, which alternates between chapters specific to the Joads' story and interchapters written with an **omniscient** narrator. He also uses his naturalistic style in descriptions of nature and the landscape, which makes the land as much a character in the story as any of the people. Descriptions of the harsh, bleak world of Dust Bowl Oklahoma and Edenic California propel the plot, presenting a deterministic view that life is driven by natural forces that are outside man's control.

The novel opens with the omniscient narrator describing the Dust Bowl conditions that drive the people from their land, then shifts the focus to the story of the Joads. Tom Joad, on parole from prison for murder, hitchhikes home. On the way he meets ex-preacher Jim Casy. Casy left the church because he has come to place his faith in people, not God, and tells Tom, "maybe that's the Holy Sperit—the human spirit … Maybe all men got one big soul ever'body's a part of."

The two make their way to the Joad farm to find it deserted. At the farm they come across a local man, Muley Graves, who has been driven off his land. Muley refuses to leave Oklahoma because the land is in his blood, so he wanders around like a "graveyard ghost'" from empty farm to empty farm, sleeping and eating when he can. Despite his poverty, Muley shares his food with Tom and Casy because "if a fella's got somepin to eat

an' another fella's hungry … the first fella ain't got no choice." Muley tells them that the Joad family is at their Uncle John's farm, preparing to leave for California.

Tom reunites with his family: Uncle John, Ma and Pa Joad, brothers Noah, Al, and Winfield, sisters Rose of Sharon (Rosasharn) and Ruthie, Granpa and Granma Joad, and Rosasharn's husband, Connie Rivers. The family confers at the truck they will take to California, which has become "the new hearth, the living center of the family," about whether they can take Casy with them on their journey west. Although the men of the family make the decisions, Ma believes they should let Casy join them because it is not in their nature to deny help to someone in need. The family agrees, and they prepare to leave for California, having sold as many of their possessions as they could and receiving practically no money for them. Granpa, the eldest Joad, does not want to leave Oklahoma, which he believes is his country. The family must drug him to get him aboard the truck.

The Joads take Highway 66, which is the "path of people in flight … the mother road," and quickly realize that the journey will be arduous. The family dog is run over when they stop at a gas station and they are initially treated with hostility by the station's owner, who assumes that they are beggars. The Joads stop to set up camp for the night and meet Ivy and Sairy Wilson, who are traveling from Kansas. When Granpa suffers a stroke, the Wilsons offer up the bed in their tent, and when he dies, Sairy helps Ma prepare him to be buried. The Joads and the Wilsons come together as one group, where "Each'll help each, an' we'll all git to California." The relationship between the families is further solidified when the Wilsons' car breaks down and the Joads offer to help fix it instead of leaving them behind. When Rosasharn talks about not wanting to live in the country in California, and Tom suggests the rest go on ahead while he and Casy fix the car, Ma seizes power and control

A Missouri migrant family in search of work stops their packed truck by the side of U.S. Highway 99 near Tracy, California.

A destitute family lives in a makeshift tent in the Neideffer Camp in Holtville, California after having sold everything they owned for food and losing a child to exposure over the winter.

over the family. She will not allow them to split up because, with no home and very few provisions, "all we got is the family unbroke."

In a roadside campground on the way, Pa Joad meets a man who tells him he is on his way back from California—that the handbills promising work were a plot to get as many workers there as possible so they can pay them smaller wages—but he does not heed the warning. Still believing that things might be different for them, the group continues on its way. When they finally reach California, they still have miles of desert to get through and they stop at the Colorado River. Here Pa meets another man who warns him about California, telling him that people like him and the Wilsons are called "Okies" and are looked down on by the people in California, and that the land is "nice to look at, but you can't have none of it."

At the river, Noah decides that he is going to leave the group. In the tent, Ma and Rosasharn tend to Granma, who has fallen ill. Their rest is

interrupted by a California lawman who tells them to be gone by morning. Ma is enraged by the man's disrespect, and the family decides to move on so they do not run in to trouble with the authorities.

In addition to the loss of Noah, the Wilsons insist that the Joads move on without them as Sairy has fallen ill. With the family falling apart, Ma rides in the back of the truck with Granma, determined that "the fambly got to get acrost," but by the time the Joads reach the fertile valleys of California, Granma has been dead for hours. Having lost three family members, as well as the Wilsons, the Joads stop at one of the Hooverville tent camps outside of town. They meet a man named Floyd Knowles, who warns Tom about the way the growers take advantage of the workers and then run them off the land after the harvest, and that if anyone tries to join together and speak out they are blacklisted and harassed by the police, ending up in jail or dead.

Ma, who is still clinging to a sense of community, offers up the Joads' extra stew to the starving children at the camp; she is later chastised by a woman for her act of kindness, which shows her that there is a sense of isolation and distrust in the camps. Connie abandons the family, and the pregnant Rosasharn, and does not return, and that evening Uncle John gets drunk on money he had been hiding from the family.

Trouble breaks out when a man comes into the camp offering work. Floyd insists that he show credentials and agree to a certain wage beforehand. The local deputy tries to arrest Floyd, but he escapes—Tom trips the deputy, and Casy takes the blame for the entire incident, which lands him in jail. The remaining Joads decide to leave the Hooverville and go to the government-run Weedpatch camp. After they leave, the authorities burn the Hooverville to prevent further unrest.

The Weedpatch government camp, in contrast to the Hooverville, is a welcoming environment for the Joads.

A group of migrant children play together at a Farm Security Administration camp near Calipatria in California's Imperial Valley.

They are provided shelter, access to medicine, and sanitary units for bathing and laundry. The flushing toilets are completely foreign to the youngest Joad children, Ruthie and Winfield. The camps are democratic and self-governed, and they are safe from the hostility of the local authorities. The manager of the camp, Jim Rawley (based on Tom Collins), welcomes Ma, who is initially suspicious of him but is soon reassured. Unlike other authority figures they have encountered, Rawley treats her with

Striking miners in Ducktown, Tennessee wait for strikebreakers called "scabs" to come out of the copper mines.

respect and she starts to "feel like people again." The camp even has a Ladies' Association and Ma is called on by a committee of three women who "walked down the road with dignity."

For the first time since they left Oklahoma, the Joads can stop moving and begin to feel settled. Only Tom is able to find work, however, since there are more workers than jobs in the area. The government camp can provide better living conditions for the migrant farmers, but the Farmers Association and the growers control employment and wages. There is an alliance between the Farmers Association and the local authorities, who are resentful that they have no control over Weedpatch. They form a plan to cause a disturbance at the camp dance so they have an excuse to raid and make arrests. The men at the camp learn of this plan beforehand, and Tom joins a group to prevent it. Working as a group, the migrants are able to defeat their oppressors, but they learn that the men sent in to start the fight were also migrant men. They were doing what they had to do to earn money.

After a month at the camp, the men are still unable to find enough work to sustain the family. As much as she enjoys the benefits of life at Weedpatch, Ma decides that the family must move on to find work. She takes complete control of the family's decision, demonstrating a shift in power from the men to the matriarch, and Pa accepts it, saying, "Time was when a man said what we'd do. Seems like women is tellin' now." They travel to the Hooper Ranch, a peach farm, and are guided in by a policeman through a crowd of striking workers. The wages for picking are horribly low but the family has no choice but to take the work, and with the whole family working they manage to make only one dollar, which buys them practically nothing at the company grocery store. The store's prices are too high, and Ma can only afford enough for one simple meal. She tells the store clerk that she is learning that "if you're in trouble or hurt or need—go to poor people. They're the only ones that'll help."

When Tom sneaks out to investigate the commotion outside the ranch, he runs into Jim Casy, who has been released from prison and has become a labor organizer. While in jail, Casy learned the effectiveness of group action and working together, and has joined in the effort to organize the migrants and strike to improve work conditions. They are discovered by authorities and Casy is killed, which sets Tom off. He kills the man who murdered Casy, sustaining injury himself, and hides. When he is able to get back to the camp, Tom tells the family what happened. They decide to leave the ranch so that Tom isn't discovered. With the strike over, wages have been dropped even lower, and there is nothing to keep them there.

Ma will not allow Tom to leave the group, and when they come across a sign advertising cotton-picking work, the Joads move into a **boxcar** they share with the Wainwright family. Tom hides in a cave nearby while the others go to work, and the family is able to bring in enough money to eat and buy some new clothes.

When Ruthie reveals Tom's secret during an argument with another child, , Ma knows that he will have to leave and she goes to his hiding place. Tom says that he has been inspired by Casy's ideas and is going to join the labor movement. After Ma says goodbye to Tom, she learns of another picking job nearby and brings the news to the boxcar. Al and Aggie Wainwright become engaged and everyone celebrates the joining of the two families. Because of the number of available workers, the cotton field is picked clean by mid-morning. The Joads and Wainwrights return to the boxcar as it begins to pour.

The rain does not stop for days and the camp begins to flood, but with Rosasharn in labor the Joads are unable to leave. Pa Joad organizes the men in the camp to build a dam and "over the men came a fury of work, a fury of battle. When one man dropped his shovel, another took it up." Though they succeed in building up the riverbank, a downed tree takes out their

A migrant family lives in a freight train car, known as a boxcar, in
Toppenish, Washington State.

dam and the camp is washed out. Pa returns to discover that Rosasharn has had a stillborn child and Uncle John is sent to bury it. With the fields too flooded, he sends the body down the stream in an apple box, as if delivering a message to the townspeople: "Go down in the street an' rot an' tell 'em that way."

The next morning the Joads know they must leave as the water continues to rise. Al stays behind with the Wainwrights, and the remaining members of the Joad family—Ma, Pa, Uncle John, Ruthie, Winfield, and Rosasharn—seek cover in a barn. They come across a sick man who is starving because he has given all his food to his son. The novel ends with an act of pure kindness, as Rosasharn feeds the stranger milk from her breast.

Cultural Context

Steinbeck provides the cultural context for the novel within the novel itself, using his interchapters to describe in poetic terms the environmental, social, and economic factors driving the migrant farmers to California. The Dust Bowl farmers were living on "scarred earth" that had been damaged by overproduction, drought, and wind, and could no longer sustain crops or livestock. The banks were foreclosing on farmers' land, and the tenant farmers were being put out since the owners did not need them when they could have one man on a tractor do all the work. Steinbeck calls the banks and the large landholders "the monster" over which individual men have no control. The depressed economy also created the opportunity for car salesmen to take advantage of the desperate farmers, who needed reliable transportation and parts to make it to the West.

The trip to California on Highway 66 was a long, dangerous journey for families in run-down cars with little money or supplies. The corporate farmers and men on tractors who had taken over the land had no connection with it. As the road became home for migrant families, they lost their

A pile of straw burns in a Crowley, Louisiana rice field during the Depression, when destruction of surplus crops was a common practice even though people were starving.

connection with the land as well. They were transient, never stopping for very long, and they lived in fear of the danger and discrimination they faced on the road.

When they arrived in California, it was not the "land of milk and honey" they were led to believe it would be. They were harassed upon entering the state and at their roadside camps because the local authorities and land owners feared that they might start a revolt—that, if allowed to form these communities, the "I" thinking would turn into "we" thinking that could allow them to fight the economic system that kept them in poverty while the Farmers Association profited. While people were starving, growers destroyed crops to keep the price up, and the people's hunger turned to anger: "in the eyes of the hungry there is a growing wrath. In the souls of the people the

grapes of wrath are filling and growing heavy, growing heavy for the vintage."

There were some programs in place to help the migrant farmers in California, such as the government-run camps set up by the Resettlement Administration, but without the cooperation of local law enforcement and the growers who set prices, there was only so much the federal programs could do. Despite the fact that labor unions had the right to strike and engage in collective bargaining, the scare tactics and intimidation used by the growers, as well as the number of migrants willing to work as strikebreakers, made any real progress in labor relations impossible. The only hope, Steinbeck suggests, is for all the downtrodden to band together as a community and organize. As individuals, they are easily taken advantage of and defeated; in a group, they become a force to be reckoned with.

Major Characters

Tom Joad

Tom Joad is a man of action throughout the novel. When he is released from prison, he has more selfish interests and wants to live for the moment. Over the course of the novel, with the influence of Jim Casy, his actions shift from a focus on himself to a focus on others. He acts in the best interest of the family, offering to fix the Wilsons' car; he acts in the interest of the community of migrants when he trips the deputy at the Hooverville. By the end of the novel he has avenged Casy's death and taken up his altruistic cause of organizing the workers, telling Ma: "Wherever they's a fight so hungry people can eat, I'll be there. Wherever they's a cop beatin' up a guy, I'll be there … An' when our folks eat the stuff they raise an' live in the houses they build—why, I'll be there." His character development represents Steinbeck's ideal solution to the problems facing Depression-era society.

Jim Casy

As a former preacher, Casy is a man of thought. At the beginning of the novel, he is trying to come to terms with his idea of what is sinful and what is holy and developing a new philosophy wherein "There ain't no sin and there ain't no virtue. There's just stuff people do. It's all part of the same thing." Casy comes to place his faith in the human spirit instead of the Holy Spirit, although he is still more of a philosopher than an activist. Over the course of the novel, Casy takes a more active role, ultimately sacrificing his freedom for Tom and his life for the cause of social justice. Jim Casy is partially based on Ed Ricketts and is a Christ-like figure in the novel, with Tom eventually becoming his disciple and taking up his message after his death.

Ma Joad

Ma is "the citadel of the family" and her unwavering goal throughout the novel is to keep the family "unbroke." Without work the men have lost their position as providers and Ma seizes control of the family. Her roles and responsibilities have not changed—now more than ever, Ma must take care of the family and make sure they stay strong. She is responsible for making a home when they no longer have a place to call their own, and she is gracious and generous to people outside the family. Ma realizes that in the harsh world they live in, only the poorest people are willing to help each other, and she takes on the added responsibility of watching out for people who are not her kin. At the end of the novel, she tells Mrs. Wainwright, "Use' ta be the fambly was fust. It ain't so now. It's anybody. Worse off we get, the more we got to do." She represents a sense of decency, kindness, and strength of the human spirit even in the worst of circumstances.

Dorothea Lange's famous photograph, known as *Migrant Mother*, depicts 32-year-old Florence Owens Thompson, a destitute mother of seven working as a pea picker in Nipomo, California, in 1936.

Major Themes

The Group vs. the Individual

The Grapes of Wrath makes distinctions between the actions of individual people and the actions of a group. The novel's main message of the benefit of collective action is clear in the way Ma strives to keep the family working together as a unit, the way the migrant communities operate better when the people work together (as in the Weedpatch camp), and the way that social justice can only be achieved through labor organization. The forces working against the migrants also work as groups: the landowners and farm associations, the banks, and the corporations. Though these entities are "the monster" that destroys the common man, they are made up of individual people whose goals and beliefs are not necessarily the same as the group they make up. Steinbeck's phalanx theory can be summed up in the way he presents the banks that foreclose on the farmers' land: "The bank is something else than men. It happens that every man in a bank hates what the bank does, and yet the bank does it. The bank is something more than men … It's the monster. Men made it, but they can't control it."

The Effects of Modernization

The rapid industrialization of the farming industry in the late nineteenth and early twentieth centuries had a devastating effect on the traditional farmer and on the land. In his quest for industrial expansion and profit,

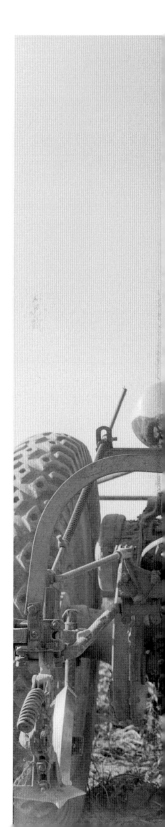

A farmer stands on a tractor while working on the New Deal farm cooperative program in the Lake Dick area of Jefferson County, Arkansas.

man tractored up large areas of the Great Plains that were not suitable for farming and planted cash crops like cotton and wheat. In the process, they destroyed the topsoil and "kill[ed] the land with cotton." In the modern world, the family farm was replaced by the corporate farm and the tenant farming system, which was no longer a viable way of life during the Depression. Economic forces combined with the natural forces of drought and wind to create the Dust Bowl conditions that drove people from "the scarred earth" to the West, where the land was fertile and unspoiled. When they arrived, they found that California was not the new Garden of Eden they had hoped it was. Though the land was bountiful, "the smell of rot fills the country"; working within the corporate farming structure, men "cannot create a system whereby their fruits may be eaten."

Industrialization also robbed people of their connection with the land. One man on a tractor, separated from the land by a machine, could do the work of many farming families. The use of machines instead of manpower makes the work "so efficient that the wonder goes out of land and the working of it, and with the wonder the deep understanding and the relation." The man hired to work the tractor does not live on the land as the farmer does and, without the respect that comes from working and living off the land, he has no appreciation for it. The migrant farmers who lost their land as a result of industrial farming practices become rootless—their cars and trucks replace the farms as their home as they travel from place to place looking for work. When they can briefly settle in the migrant camps, neither the land they live on nor the land they work belongs to them. To Steinbeck, who placed a great deal of value in the environment and the natural world, the losses suffered by the traditional farmer in the modern world demonstrated "a failure that topples all our successes."

A wild painted turtle crosses a road in Redding, California.

Major Symbol: The Turtle

The land turtle in Chapter 3 is symbolic of the migrant farmers' struggles as they journey west. It carries its home on its back as it makes its way past obstacles to cross the highway. Crossing the road, it experiences both kindness (in the woman who swerves not to hit it) and cruelty (as the truck driver who hits it on purpose). Flipped on its back by the truck, the turtle struggles to right itself again and continues on its journey. The turtle's single-minded determination to continue on its path despite all obstacles thrown in its way is symbolic of the strength of the human spirit to carry on despite adversity.

Timeline

1902 John Ernst Steinbeck born February 27 in Salinas, California.

1917 The United States enters World War I.

1919 Treaty of Versailles ends World War I; Steinbeck enters Stanford, where he will attend classes on and off for six years, and begins to work various jobs for Spreckels Sugar.

1925 Steinbeck leaves Stanford without completing his degree and works as a laborer during the construction of Madison Square Garden in New York City.

1929 *Cup of Gold* is published; Herbert Hoover becomes 31st President of the United States; the stock market crashes and America enters the Great Depression.

1930 Steinbeck marries Carol Henning and meets Ed Ricketts; Smoot-Hawley Tariff Act is passed.

1931 Severe drought conditions in the Great Plains dry out the land and dust storms begin; food riots break out across the U.S.

1932 *The Pastures of Heaven* is published; Herbert Hoover loses reelection bid.

1933 Franklin Delano Roosevelt becomes 32nd President of the United States and launches many New Deal programs

during his first hundred days; *To a God Unknown* is published; San Joaquin Valley cotton workers strike.

1934 Drought becomes worst in U.S. history, affecting twenty-seven states.

1935 *Tortilla Flat* is published by Pat Covici, with whom Steinbeck will work for the rest of his life; worst "black blizzard" of the Dust Bowl (known as Black Sunday) occurs; FDR launches Second New Deal programs.

1936 *In Dubious Battle* is published; Steinbeck travels to California's Hoovervilles and the government-run camp at Arvin, where he meets Resettlement Administration official Tom Collins; "The Harvest Gypsies" articles are published in *The San Francisco News*; FDR elected to a second term.

1937 *Of Mice and Men* and *The Red Pony* are published.

1938 *Their Blood Is Strong* and *The Long Valley* are published; Steinbeck witnesses flood conditions in Visalia, California.

1939 *The Grapes of Wrath* is published; the drought ends.

1940 FDR elected to a third term; Steinbeck takes boat expedition to the Gulf of California with Ed Ricketts.

Timeline

1941 Japanese bomb Pearl Harbor, Hawaii, and the United States enters World War II; the Great Depression ends; Steinbeck separates from Carol Henning and moves in with Gwyn Conger; *Sea of Cortez* is published.

1942 *The Moon Is Down* and *Bombs Away* are published.

1943 Steinbeck marries Gwyn Conger; travels to Europe and North Africa as war correspondent.

1944 Thom Steinbeck is born; FDR elected to fourth term.

1945 *Cannery Row* is published; FDR dies on April 12 and Vice President Harry S. Truman becomes 33rd President; U.S. bombs Hiroshima and Nagasaki, Japan; World War II ends.

1946 John Steinbeck IV is born.

1947 *The Wayward Bus* and *The Pearl* are published; the Cold War begins.

1948 Steinbeck's divorce from Gwyn Conger is finalized; Ed Ricketts dies; *A Russian Journal* is published.

1950 *Burning Bright* is published; Steinbeck marries Elaine Scott; the United States enters the Korean War.

1952 *East of Eden* is published.

1953 Dwight D. Eisenhower becomes 34th President of the United States; Korean War ends.

1954 *Sweet Thursday* is published.

1957 *The Short Reign of Pippin IV* is published.

1960 Steinbeck tours America with his poodle, Charley.

1961 John F. Kennedy becomes 35th President of the United States; *The Winter of Our Discontent* is published.

1962 *Travels With Charley* is published; Steinbeck wins the Nobel Prize for Literature; Cuban Missile Crisis occurs.

1963 President Kennedy is assassinated and Vice President Lyndon B. Johnson becomes 36th President of the United States.

1964 Steinbeck is awarded the Presidential Medal of Freedom by President Johnson; beginning of period of major U.S. involvement in the Vietnam War.

1966 *America for Americans* is published; Steinbeck travels to Vietnam as war correspondent.

1968 Steinbeck dies from heart failure on December 20.

Steinbeck's Most Important Works

Novels and Novellas

Cup of Gold (1929)
The Pastures of Heaven (1932)
To a God Unknown (1933)
Tortilla Flat (1935)
In Dubious Battle (1936)
Of Mice and Men (1937)
The Long Valley (1938)
The Grapes of Wrath (1939)
The Moon Is Down (1942)
The Red Pony (1945)
Cannery Row (1945)
The Wayward Bus (1947)
The Pearl (1947)
Burning Bright (1950)
East of Eden (1952)
Sweet Thursday (1954)
The Short Reign of Pippin IV (1957)
The Winter of Our Discontent (1961)

Nonfiction

Their Blood Is Strong (1938)

Sea of Cortez (1941), with Edward F. Ricketts

Bombs Away (1942)

A Russian Journal (1948), with Robert Capa

The Log from the Sea of Cortez (1951)

Once There Was a War (1958)

Travels With Charley in Search of America (1962)

America and Americans (1966)

Glossary

bindle stiff
A transient who carries his possessions and bedding in a bundle.

boxcar
A section of a train that has a roof and large, sliding doors and that carries goods and supplies.

breadline
A line of people waiting to receive free food or other relief.

bunkhouse
A building where workers sleep.

collective bargaining
Negotiations between an employer and a labor union regarding wages, hours, and/or working conditions.

Communist
An individual or political party believing in a system of government in which the state plans and controls the economy and a single, often authoritarian party holds power, claiming to make progress toward a higher social order in which all goods are equally shared by the people.

determinism
The belief that occurrences in nature, social phenomena, and acts of man are determined by preceding events or natural forces.

ecology
A science that deals with the relationships between groups of living things and their environments.

handbill
A small printed advertisement or announcement that is given out to many people by hand.

margin call
A demand by a broker that an investor deposit more money to cover possible losses.

naturalism
A theory or practice in literature that emphasizes scientific observation of life without idealization and often including elements of determinism.

non-teleological
A way of viewing the world that examines what is instead of what could be or should be, and which asks what and how but not why.

novella
Short novel, also "novelette."

omniscient
Having unlimited knowledge and understanding.

Glossary

paisanos
People of mixed Spanish, Indian, Mexican, and Caucasian descent.

phalanx theory
Steinbeck's theory that a group made up of individual units takes on the characteristics of an individual and is stronger than the sum of its parts.

polio
A disease that affects the nerves of the spine and often makes a person permanently unable to move particular muscles.

pseudonym
A false name, often a pen name.

sharecropper
A farmer who raises crops for a land owner and is paid a portion of the money from the sale of the crops.

stable buck
A derogatory term for a man (usually for an African American) who works and sleeps in a stable.

subsidies
Money that is paid (usually by a government) to keep the price of a product or service low or to help a business or organization continue to function.

tariff
A tax on goods coming into or leaving a country.

teleological
A way of viewing the world that looks for a cause,
design, and/or purpose (often spiritual or supernatural)
in observable phenomena.

tenant farmer
A farmer who raises crops on land owned by someone else
and pays rent either in the form of money or a share of the
crops produced.

topsoil
The upper layer of soil in which plants have most of their roots
and which a farmer turns over in plowing.

Sources

Introduction

P. 5: Steinbeck, John, *Steinbeck: A Life in Letters*, edited by Elaine Steinbeck and Robert Wallstein, (New York, NY: Penguin Books, 1989), p.75.

P. 7: Steinbeck, *Steinbeck: A Life in Letters*, edited by Elaine Steinbeck and Robert Wallstein, p.898.

P. 7: Steinbeck, *Steinbeck: A Life in Letters*, edited by Elaine Steinbeck and Robert Wallstein, p.898.

Chapter 1

P. 12: Hoover, Herbert ,"The President's News Conference, Washington, D.C., November 15, 1929." www.presidency. ucsb.edu/ws/index.php?pid=22005

P. 16: Roosevelt, Franklin Delano, "Address Accepting the Presidential Nomination at the Democratic National Convention," Chicago, Illinois, July 2, 1932. www.presidency. ucsb.edu/ws/?pid=75174

Chapter 2

P. 34: Steinbeck, *Steinbeck: A Life in Letters*, edited by Elaine Steinbeck and Robert Wallstein, p.15.

P. 38: Steinbeck, *Steinbeck: A Life in Letters*, edited by Elaine Steinbeck and Robert Wallstein, p.76.

P. 51: Steinbeck, *Steinbeck: A Life in Letters,* edited by Elaine Steinbeck and Robert Wallstein, p.898.

Chapter 3

All quotations from *Of Mice and Men* are from the 1993 Penguin edition.

Chapter 4

All quotations from *The Grapes of Wrath* are from the 2006 Penguin edition.

Further Information

Books

Burkhead, Cynthia. *Student Companion to John Steinbeck.* Westport, CT: Greenwood Press, 2002.

Himmelberg, Robert F. *The Great Depression and the New Deal.* Westport, CT: Greenwood Press, 2001.

McArthur, Debra. *John Steinbeck: The Grapes of Wrath and Of Mice and Men.* Tarrytown, NY: Marshall Cavendish Benchmark, 2009.

Rauchway, Eric. *The Great Depression & the New Deal: A Very Short Introduction.* New York, NY: Oxford University Press, 2008.

Websites

Digital History: Great Depression
www.digitalhistory.uh.edu/era.cfm?eraID=14&smtID=2

PBS: Ken Burns's *The Dust Bowl*
www.pbs.org/kenburns/dustbowl

The Martha Heasley Cox Center for Steinbeck Studies
as.sjsu.edu/steinbeck/index.jsp

The Steinbeck Institute
www.steinbeckinstitute.org

Bibliography

Benson, Jackson J. *John Steinbeck, Writer*. New York, NY: Penguin Books, 1984.

Burkhead, Cynthia. *Student Companion to John Steinbeck*. Westport, CT: Greenwood Press, 2002.

Coers, Donald V., Paul D. Ruffin, and Robert J. DeMott, eds. *After The Grapes of Wrath: Essays on John Steinbeck in Honor of Tetsumaro Hayashi*. Athens, OH: Ohio University Press, 1995.

Himmelberg, Robert F. *The Great Depression and the New Deal*. Westport, CT: Greenwood Press, 2001.

Johnson, Claudia Durst. *Understanding Of Mice and Men, The Red Pony, and The Pearl: A Student Casebook to Issues, Sources, and Historical Documents*. Westport, CT: Greenwood Press, 1997.

Johnson, Claudia Durst. *Understanding The Grapes of Wrath: A Student Casebook to Issues, Sources, and Historical Documents*. Westport, CT: Greenwood Press, 1999.

Kyvig, David E. *Daily Life in the United States: 1920–1940*. Chicago, IL: Ivan R. Dee, 2004.

McArthur, Debra. *John Steinbeck: The Grapes of Wrath and Of Mice and Men*. Tarrytown, NY: Marshall Cavendish Benchmark, 2009.

McElvaine, Robert S. *The Great Depression: America, 1929–1941*. New York, NY: Three Rivers Press, 2009.

Railsback, Brian, and Michael J. Meyer, eds. *A John Steinbeck Encyclopedia*. Westport, CT: Greenwood Press, 2006.

Rauchway, Eric. *The Great Depression & the New Deal: A Very Short Introduction*. New York, NY: Oxford University Press, 2008.

Shuman, R. Baird, ed. *Great American Writers: Twentieth Century*. Vol. 11. New York: Marshall Cavendish, 2002.

Steinbeck, John. *Steinbeck: A Life in Letters*. (Elaine Steinbeck and Robert Wallstein, eds.) New York, NY: Penguin Books, 1989.

Steinbeck, John. *Of Mice and Men*. New York, NY: Penguin Books, 1993.

Steinbeck, John. *The Grapes of Wrath*. New York, NY: Penguin Classics, 2006.

Steinbeck, John. *The Harvest Gypsies*. Berkeley, CA and Santa Clara, CA: Heyday and Santa Clara University Press, 2011.

Steinbeck, John. *Working Days: The Journals of The Grapes of Wrath*. (Robert DeMott, ed.) New York, NY: Penguin Books, 1989.

Index